Pregnancy Guide

A month by month pregnancy guide for first time moms, with all the helpful tips and information that you need!

Table Of Contents

Introduction 1

Chapter 1: Pregnancy Basics.. 2

Chapter 2: First Month Of Pregnancy 7

Chapter 3: Second Month Of Pregnancy 11

Chapter 4: Third Month Of Pregnancy 13

Chapter 5: Fourth Month Of Pregnancy 15

Chapter 6: Fifth Month Of Pregnancy................................... 18

Chapter 7: Sixth Month Of Pregnancy 21

Chapter 8: Seventh Month Of Pregnancy 25

Chapter 9: Eighth Month Of Pregnancy 27

Chapter 10: Ninth Month Of Pregnancy 29

Conclusion 31

Introduction

I want to thank you and congratulate you for downloading the book, "Pregnancy Guide".

This book contains helpful information about pregnancy, and what to expect in each trimester.

The pregnancy process has been broken down into month by month phases within this book. Under each month of the pregnancy, the individual weeks are explained.

You will learn what to expect at each week of your pregnancy, and be provided with updates on how your baby is progressing with its growth and development at each stage.

Included in this book are the most common symptoms you will notice during each month. Solutions and remedies for discomforts and negative symptoms that you will experience are also provided.

This book details the steps and strategies required to successfully go through each stage of your pregnancy, and ultimately have a healthy child.

I wish you the best of luck with your pregnancy, and hope this book is able to help you!

Thanks again for downloading this book, I hope you enjoy it!

Chapter 1:
Pregnancy Basics

Pregnancy

Do you think you might be pregnant? It is always not accurate to assume, so the only way you can really confirm if you are pregnant or not is to take a pregnancy test. However, there are early pregnancy symptoms that may indicate the possibility.

There are general pregnancy symptoms, yes, but they are different for every woman. No two women will experience similar symptoms. It is also important to take note that the symptoms may manifest before and during your period, and these symptoms are often mistaken for pre-menstrual and menstrual symptoms. There are medical conditions that may also be present; hence, it is imperative that you get a test done.

Possible Spotting and Cramping

A few days after conception, the fertilized egg will attach itself to your uterus wall. When this happens, it can cause spotting, one of the earliest signs of pregnancy. It may come with cramping, but it is not a common occurrence. Doctors call this *implantation bleeding*. This may be experienced from 6 to 12 days after fertilization.

Cramps might resemble menstrual cramps so most women assume that the bleeding is just the beginning of their period.

Aside from bleeding, a white, milky discharge from the vagina may be noticeable. This is because of the thickening of the vaginal walls, which can happen almost immediately after conception. The cells that are growing on the vaginal lining are causing the discharge. This discharge may continue for the duration of the pregnancy, and it is harmless and does not require any kind of treatment. However, the discharge may emit a foul-smelling odor. You will also feel a burning sensation, as well as itchiness. Should you experience this, make sure you immediately inform your doctor because this might also indicate the presence of bacterial or a yeast infection.

Changes in the Breasts

Another early symptom of pregnancy is the feeling of soreness of the breasts. They may also become swollen and tingly to the touch from one to two weeks after conception. This is due to the hormonal changes that are beginning to take place. The breasts may also feel tender to the touch. You will begin to notice that they have become fuller and heavier. Often, the areola may also darken.

Extreme Fatigue

Feeling more tired than usual is a common occurrence during the whole period of pregnancy. Your doctor will give you vitamins and supplements in order to help offset the feelings of fatigue.

Morning Sickness and Food Cravings

Morning sickness or nausea is a popular sign of pregnancy; however, not every pregnant woman experiences it. Doctors still are yet to find out the cause of morning sickness, but they assume that changes in the level of the hormones are a huge contributor.

There are expectant moms who develop cravings for foods, and most often, they crave for foods that they used to hate.

This is also attributed to the hormonal changes within the body of a pregnant woman.

However, morning sickness and food cravings are highly likely to taper down going into the 13th or 14th week of pregnancy.

Missing the Menstrual Period

It is an obvious early pregnancy symptom. The reason why women often suspect pregnancy is missing their monthly periods.

Stages of Pregnancy :

First Trimester

The first trimester is often the most difficult. You do not look pregnant yet but you begin to feel bloated. Flatulence is also common. You easily get tired from even the lightest of movements or tasks.

During this time, your baby undergoes some changes, from being a *zygote* or a single fertilized egg; it will grow into an *embryo* implanted into your uterine wall. It will looks like a peach-sized bundle with growing limbs and body systems. First trimester milestones include the production of white blood cells that will fight off germs and bacteria, development of the baby's vocal cords, and muscle formation.

There will also be a few changes in you during the first trimester. You might experience morning sickness. This will be characterized by body malaise and nausea or vomiting. By the time you reach the 6th week, you'll experience extreme mood swings.

Second Trimester

During the next three months, there will be a lot of changes to the growing baby inside you. It will be good to for you to know that most of the uncomfortable pregnancy symptoms you experienced during the first trimester will slowly disappear.

Your growing baby will be "busy" during these months. Hair will begin to grow, their eyes and ears will be moving into their right positions, and they will begin to suck and swallow.

As you enter the 18th week, they might weigh as much as one chicken breast. They may begin to yawn. Tiny fingertips may begin to take shape.

They will continue to grow towards the end of the third trimester, and the arms and the legs may begin to grow and a few jabs and kicks might be felt. Your growing baby will also begin to develop the five senses: taste, touch, smell, hearing, and sight.

As for you, it is possible that you may still feel constipated most of the time but frequent peeing will cease. You will still feel the heartburn. You may also develop a huge appetite around this time.

Your sex drive might also decrease.

Third Trimester

During this time, your stomach may be about 2/3 of the way, but your baby still has a lot of growing up to do. Your baby may have grown to about 2 ½ lbs and about 17 in long. They may have also started to blink. During this time, they may have the ability to dream. They may also have the ability to regulate their own body temperature.

The third trimester will also be the time when your baby has fully-developed senses. They may be able to hear the sound of your voice. They are most likely able to distinguish light from dark; and this may also be the time when they are able to taste.

Their skin will also become opaque. You will also be experiencing a few pokes and kicks on your belly every now and then.

Around this time too, the baby may begin to develop the genitalia, so this is the perfect time to determine the gender of the baby through ultrasound.

You are almost at the end of the pregnancy so you will begin to feel discomfort in your abdominal area. Expect back and abdominal aches because the baby might have reached its full birth size. You will also notice the appearance of stretch marks and varicose veins.

The succeeding chapters will give you a month-by-month guide to help you through the process.

Chapter 2:
First Month Of Pregnancy

You will now receive a monthly guide to help you cope with the changes and the process itself. For each month, you will read about the changes in both the baby and yourself that you need to take note of. You will also be given answers to some of the most common issues that may arise each month and will be provided with action items and possible remedies should problems arise.

We begin with the first month.

Fetal Growth

Weeks 1 and 2

The average gestation period is 266 days, meaning, your baby will come out approximately 38 weeks after conception. Not many women are familiar with their fertility cycles and most often they fail to recognize when the conception actually occurred. Doctors generally look into the first day of the woman's last menstrual period to determine conception date.

On the average, the length of pregnancy is 280 days; this means that your baby will be born 40 weeks after the first day of your last menstrual period. Using this standard, doctors say that the first two weeks of pregnancy is actually before the child is conceived.

Week 3

This is the time when the egg and the sperm meet. Cell division process happens as the baby begins to take its form. It is also around this time the fetus' heart begin to pump blood on its own.

Week 4

As the egg undergoes division and growth, the cells begin to specialize. The fertilized egg begins its growth: the placenta develops and the amniotic sac begins to form.

About 10 days after fertilization, the fetus implants itself into your uterus. The baby's heart, lungs, and spinal cord start to develop. By the end of the first month, the baby could be less than 0.03 oz and the length could be about 1/8 of an inch.

Confirming the Pregnancy

Here are some of the steps to undertake to confirm the pregnancy:

- Pregnancy Test – You need to undergo testing for the presence of the Human Chorionic Gonadotropin (HCG) hormone in the urine 14 days from gestation.

- Enlargement of the Uterine Walls – The midwife or gynecologist will perform a vaginal exam to determine uterine enlargement. It can be detected 7 to 8 weeks into the pregnancy or 5 to 7 weeks of the gestation period. At 12 weeks, your doctor can detect the enlargement of the uterine walls via an abdominal exam. Your uterus continues to enlarge as you progress with your pregnancy.

- Cervical Softening – This is determined by performing a vaginal exam. When you reach around 8 weeks of your pregnancy or 6 weeks gestation, there will be visible discoloration and softening of your cervix.

Your pregnancy is established when:

- Doctors detect fetal heart tones using a Doppler ultrasound device. This machine can detect the fetus's heartbeat by 10 weeks gestation or 12 weeks into the pregnancy.

- You can feel the baby's parts through the abdomen. This happens about 26 weeks into the pregnancy or 24 weeks gestation.

- The baby becomes visible through ultrasound images.

Changes in Your Body

As the baby begins to grow, your body will also undergo a lot of changes. Your doctor will be requiring you to eat healthy and stay active, but you will also need to take the rest that you need.

Once the egg is fertilized, your body's production of progesterone will increase to prevent menstruation. As levels of progesterone are increased, blood supply to your uterus will increase and the uterine lining will thicken. The cervix will produce mucus to form a protective barrier. The uterus will expand and soften to give way to implantation.

You might experience cramping similar to PMS. You will also be urinating more frequently. Pregnancy hormones will cause the stimulation of the mammary glands, so you'll feel your breasts become more tender and painful at times.

Common Issues

You are likely to experience some of these during the first month:

- Increased frequency of urination
- Soreness of the breasts
- Fatigue and body malaise
- Nausea and vomiting
- Decreased sex drive
- Faintness

What to Do

- Eat healthy foods.
- Work with your doctor and ask for tips.
- Begin an appropriate exercise regimen (if you have are not into physical fitness).

Chapter 3:
Second Month Of Pregnancy

Fetal Growth

Week 6

The baby in your womb has already grown three times its original size at week 6. The limbs are beginning to develop, and the eyes and ears are starting to form.

Week 7

The baby's arms and leg buds continue to grow. Though there are no fingers yet, the shoulders begin to form. The nostrils and the eyes continue to form. The umbilical cord continues to increase in length and the baby's heart begins to bulge out of the chest.

Week 8

The baby's organs start developing. The bronchial cubes are starting to form branches and the bones are beginning to form and harden. The baby's pituitary gland is starting to develop, and the gonads are forming into either ovaries or testes. When week 8 ends, all of the vital organs have developed. The brain and spinal column also continue in their development.

Changes in Your Body

When you enter your 2nd month, the active pregnancy hormones have caused further growth of your breasts. Morning sickness may be experienced. Overall, your body begins to require more energy-boosting foods.

The volume of blood that your body produces may have increased in order to meet the needs of your growing baby. Your vagina might be swollen and extra sensitive because of the increased blood supply. There will also be more vaginal discharge to ensure that the area is clean and free from infection.

You will experience mood swings, which may be due to the hormonal changes.

Common Issues

- Soreness and heaviness of the breasts
- Increased urination
- Fatigue
- Extreme mood changes
- Faintness
- Morning sickness
- Increased vaginal discharge

What to Do

- Continue eating the right foods.
- Regular visits to your doctor.
- Take vitamin supplements as recommended by your doctor.
- Perform light exercises.

Chapter 4:
Third Month Of Pregnancy

Growth Progress

Week 9

The baby's digestive organs and reproductive organs begin to form. However, the gender is not yet detected as the genitalia are not yet fully developed. The gallbladder, pancreas, and bile ducts have formed.

Week 10

The lips have fully formed. The tooth buds begin to appear in the gums. The baby's brain is developing.

Week 11

The baby in your womb has taken a more human-like form. Fingernails begin to appear. Their eyes continue to develop, forming the iris around this time. The blood vessels in the placenta increase in size to ensure that more nutrients are provided for the baby's growth.

Week 12

The face begins to form at this time. All the 32 teeth buds have been completely formed. The nails on the fingers and the toes begin to take their form. The pituitary gland begins to produce hormones. The placenta becomes mature enough to absorb more pregnancy hormones.

Week 13

Your developing baby begins to have a more defined face. The eyes begin to take their proper position. Around this time, movements begin to unveil, like the baby sucking their thumb in their mouth. The bones in the head begin to form.

Changes in Your Body

You will notice that you are gaining weight to accommodate the baby. It is normal for pregnant women to gain extra pounds.

By the end of the third month, fluctuations in your hormone levels may have decreased, and the mood swings will begin to fade away. This is a crucial month because there is a risk in having a miscarriage.

Common Issues

- Increased vaginal discharge.
- Morning sickness.
- Increased body weight.
- Mood swings (but beginning to decrease).

What to Do

- You might experience worst cases of nausea and vomiting during this period so you have to take extra care of what you eat.
- This month could also be your first prenatal check up.

Chapter 5:
Fourth Month Of Pregnancy

Growth Progress

Week 14

As your baby continues to grow, the thyroid matures around this time and it begins to produce hormones. Its digestive system is also mature enough to produce and remove urine, which goes out into the amniotic fluid. The baby is also beginning to learn how to breathe.

Week 15

The eyes and ears of the baby are almost in their right position around this time. The hair follicles begin to grow some hair and a pattern starts to develop on the scalp. The baby's muscles and bones continue to develop. They are also able to curl up their fingers to make a first.

Week 16

The baby inside you begins to gain control of its movements. It begins to make facial expressions as its way of responding to activities in the uterine environment. Your baby's heartbeat can now be detected with the use of a regular stethoscope. The baby will be making movements inside, but a first-time mom won't be able to feel them yet.

Week 17

Your placenta continues to grow as your baby grows bigger. The baby develops "brown fat" to help maintain the right body temperature. This special type of fat can make up 2.5% of its total weight at birth, but it will be eliminated after birth.

Changes in Your Body

You will notice some veins are becoming more prominent, particularly around the legs, and your nipples may have started to darken. You might also notice red marks or blemishes on your face. Some of your major organs begin to work twice as hard in order to keep up with the needs of both you and the growing baby. The baby makes a few movements but you may or may not recognize the movements. Often, first time moms feel like "butterflies are fluttering" in their stomach.

Common Issues and What You Can Do

- Heartburn – Practice eating smaller and frequent meals. Drink plenty of liquid. Eat more foods with fiber.

- Skin blotching – Because of high hormone levels, you may get blotches on your face or darkening of the underarm and other areas. Avoid being out in the sun too much because that will make the blotches darken. Add foods with folic acid in your diet.

- Increased fatigue – Make sure that you eat enough foods that will give you energy. Get some exercise daily. Get enough rest.

- Vaginal discharge - Wear comfortable, cotton panties. Avoid wearing tight undergarments and pants/shorts. Wear panty linger to help control moisture. Continue to observe proper hygiene. Some women recommend not wearing panties when you sleep to allow the skin around the vagina to dry out. If you suspect an infection, consult your doctor immediately

Others

- It is imperative that you continue to follow a proper diet plan.

- Exercise is important to stay healthy. However, you should consult with your doctor for safety concerns.

- As your belly begins to show, you need to start wearing proper maternity clothing.

Chapter 6:
Fifth Month Of Pregnancy

Growth Progress

Week 18

During this week, your baby might begin to see and hear. They begin to distinguish light from darkness. While the sounds that they hear are still muffled, being inside with the amniotic fluid around them, the baby begins to recognize your voice and the other voices in the household.

Week 19

The baby has developed two distinct skin protections: *vernix caseosa* and *lanugo hair*. *Vernix caseosa* is a thick and white creamy substance that prevents the amniotic fluid to cause damage to your baby's skin. This layer will wear off before the baby is born. *Lanugo hair,* on the other hand, develops all over the baby's body. It will also disappear before you give birth.

Week 20

The baby's skin begins to develop the layers that will protect their bones and other body tissues. The kidneys begin to function to produce urine.

Week 21

As the baby's bones continue to harden, the bone marrow begins to develop.

Changes in Your Body

While your nausea and vomiting have disappeared, you may begin to experience indigestion and heartburn. Your belly continues to grow to accommodate the baby, and stretch marks might develop.

The thyroid gland becomes more active so you might perspire more than usual.

Common Issues and What You Can Do

- Heartburn – Try eating smaller meals to decrease the pressure on the digestive system. This will help in the digestion process. Eat smaller and more frequent meals; you don't need to follow the traditional three-meal schedule. Drink more water and add more fiber to your diet. Drink peppermint tea.

- Quickening – This refers to the times when you feel your baby moving. The movements will not hurt you or the baby, and it doesn't hurt if you push the baby back gently, as if you are playing with them. If the baby's kicks become uncomfortable, try shifting your position or walk a little to shift the baby's position a little.

- Stretch marks – Stay hydrated and eat foods that are rich in vitamins C and E to keep the skin healthy. Apply moisturizer on your skin.

- Nosebleeds – Pinch your nose when you experience this and lean forward a little to stop the bleeding. Include foods rich in vitamin C in your diet to promote healing and good tissue heath. Some women rub a small amount of petroleum jelly on their nostril before sleeping.

- Vaginal discharge – In addition, clean your vagina using a clean cloth and warm water only. Do not use soap or other non-hypoallergenic products. You can ask your gynecologist for some recommendations. Decrease sugar in your diet.

- Constipation – The increased levels of progesterone can cause the digestive system to become sluggish, thus resulting in drier and harder feces because more water is re-absorbed rather than eliminated. You can increase water intake. Adding more fibrous foods in your diet is also beneficial. Eat more fresh, raw fruits and vegetables. Drink prune juice or eat prunes every day. Add whole grains and complex carbohydrates to your daily menu plan. Cut down on caffeine.

- Pelvic pain – As your baby grows, so does your belly, and this often results in pelvic pain. Try maintaining proper posture. Exercise to keep the core muscles strong and keep your pelvis properly aligned. You can apply a hot compress on the pelvic area to relieve pain or you can have the area massaged.

- Varicose veins – Perform exercises on your legs and feet to improve blood circulation. When you need to be on your feet for longer amounts of time, make sure to take frequent rest periods. Avoid wearing clothing that restricts movement. Whenever you can, sit in the cross-legged position. Massage the legs and feet regularly using aromatic oil. It is inevitable to gain weight when you're pregnant, just make sure that you are eating healthy.

Chapter 7:
Sixth Month Of Pregnancy

Growth Progress

Week 22

By this time, the baby has developed an additional two senses, the sense of touch and sense of taste. All the essential body organ systems are in their proper places, as maturation and specialization of the systems continue. If you are going to have a baby girl, her reproductive organs are beginning to form in their proper positions. If it's a boy, the testes are starting to descend from his abdomen.

Week 23

The baby's bones in the middle ear are beginning to harden, this is necessary for the baby to develop proper hearing and have good balance. As the ear continues to develop, the baby in your womb will begin to respond to the sounds and noise that it hears from the outside.

Week 24

Your baby continues to grow and their lungs begin to produce surfactant which is needed by the lungs to perform its functions. This substance will ensure that the walls of the lungs do not stick with each other when the baby exhales. The development of the lungs takes longer compared to the other major body organs, and it will not be completed until the baby is born.

While the baby's body size has caught up with the size of his head, it is still large compared to that of an average adult, but the baby's head and body are in the right proportions for newborns. By the end of week 24, the baby will be weighing almost 2lbs and measure around 10in from crown to rump.

Week 25

Your baby's spine begins to take shape around this time. The spine is an integral part because it helps support the baby in upright positions. The muscles and bones in its hands have developed and they can now clench their fingers into a fist.

Week 26

You baby's eyes begin to open and close and start to see through the amniotic fluid.

Changes in Your Body

This is the second trimester and there are many changes taking place in your body. The uterus is now too large for the pelvis, thus there is less pressure exerted on the bladder. However, the uterus is still not quite large enough to have negative effects on your regular breathing and other functions.

You will have more energy now compared to the previous stage, so expect to gain even more weight. The thyroid gland continues to be active, thus causing you to perspire even more.

Some expectant moms begin to experience leaking from their breasts, this is normal because the mammary glands are beginning to work to produce milk, but it is also normal for the breasts not to leak.

Common Issues and What You Can Do

- Heartburn and indigestion – Keep track of what you eat and make sure you have a well-balanced diet. Consult your doctor for recommendations.

- Constipation

- Possible bladder infections – The pressure of the growing uterus and the increased metabolic rate cause frequent urination. You still need to drink more water. While this may not decrease your frequent trips to the bathroom, it ensures that you don't experience discomfort and fatigue. You can add lemon to your drinking water to increase the acidity of your urine. If you feel like peeing, do not hold it in and just go ahead. Wear cotton panties.

- Stretch marks

- Skin blotching

- Varicose veins

- Vaginal discharge

- Weight gain

- Leg cramps – Eat calcium-rich foods. Avoid wearing clothes that are too tight, especially if restricting blood flow to the legs. Take constant walks to improve blood circulation. Massage your legs with oil infused with basil. If your job requires you to sit often, take short breaks to stretch your legs.

- Difficulty breathing – If you experience shortness of breath, change positions. When you sleep, add extra pillows so that you can maintain a position where you can breathe easily. Avoid eating heavy meals, especially before going to bed.

Chapter 8:
Seventh Month Of Pregnancy

Growth Progress

Week 27

At this point, the baby's brain growth will escalate even more. Their immune system continues to improve. The liver and the lungs continue to mature and develop.

Week 28

Your baby's brain continues to develop as brain tissues increase and the make-up continues to mature.

Week 29

The baby keeps on growing. When you get an ultrasound image, you will be able to see it forming into a full-grown newborn baby.

Week 30

The baby begins to move their muscles. The lungs keep on building a steady supply of surfactant. Doctors say that the surfactant contains a kind of protein that triggers hormonal changes in both you and your baby. These changes are the early stages of your body getting ready for the birth of your child.

Common Issues and What You Can Do

- Fatigue

- Heartburn

- Constipation and indigestion

- Stretch marks

- Varicose veins

- Backache – Have someone massage your back. Perform light exercises. You might want to try pregnancy yoga. Avoid wearing high-heeled shoes.

- Cramps

- Nosebleeds

- Skin discoloration

- Vaginal discharge

- Swelling – This is a normal occurrence during pregnancy. Make sure you increase your fluid intake. Do not wear tight clothing. Exercise.

- Breast leakage

- Sleep problems – When you begin to have trouble sleeping, use more pillows to support your stomach, back, and your legs. Ask someone for a gentle yet relaxing massage to help you transition into sleep. Take a warm shower before going to bed. Exercise regularly. Since you are no longer sensitive to smells, you can light aromatic candles in your bedroom to help you relax. Drink chamomile tea prior to sleeping.

Chapter 9:
Eighth Month Of Pregnancy

Growth Progress

Week 31

Your baby is almost fully developed and you are only waiting for your due date.

Week 32

All of the five senses are fully functioning at this time. There are more movements going on.

Week 33

The baby is beginning to sleep a lot inside of you.

Week 34

The baby's body is now mature. The lungs are almost fully developed. The lanugo hair has almost disappeared and the vernix is thicker around this time. Its fingernails have grown and they pass out about one pint of fluid daily.

Week 35

Around this time, the baby seems to be gaining a lot of weight. At an average, babies weigh about 5.5 lbs at 35 weeks.

Common Issues and What You Can Do

- Fatigue

- Heartburn

- Stretch marks

- Pelvic and back pain

- Varicose veins

- Leg cramps

- Contractions – If you are moving around when the contractions occur, try to sit still and change your activity. Drink water. Eat something; contractions normally happen around this time if the baby is hungry. Relax.

- Shortness of breath

- Decreased sex drive – This is normal and you and your spouse should talk about this especially if you don't feel comfortable having intercourse. However, doctors recommend sex because it is a form of exercise. You can try new positions to ease pressure on your belly and back.

Chapter 10:
Ninth Month Of Pregnancy

Growth Progress

Week 36

The baby could be weighing between 3 and 6.5 lbs.

Week 37

By this time, the baby's lungs are almost mature and they continue to practice breathing. Their brain and muscle development are almost complete. Your baby is able to grasp with its fingers.

Week 38

If you are having a baby boy, the testicles have completely descended into the scrotum at this time. If it's a girl, her labia are fully developed. The baby will begin to eliminate its first bowel movements, called the meconium.

Week 39

You are almost ready for delivery. The lanugo hair is completely gone and the vernix is starting to disappear.

Week 40

The baby is almost ready to be born. It now weighs around 6 to 8 lbs.

Common Issues

- Breast swelling
- Fatigue
- Constipation
- Cramps
- Nausea
- Pelvic pressure and pain
- Sleep problems
- Nosebleeds
- Heartburn
- Decreased interest in sex
- Frequent urination

What You Need to Do

Since you are almost ready for delivery, you need to get a lot of rest and continue eating a well-balanced diet. Continue to perform pregnancy exercises to make the delivery less difficult.

This is the perfect time to get more information about what to expect during delivery and how you can cope afterwards.

Amidst all the preparations for the coming of the baby, you need to ensure that you get enough rest and sleep to prepare yourself for delivery.

Conclusion

Thank you again for downloading this book!

I hope this book was able to help you learn more about the different stages of pregnancy!

The next step is to put this information to use, and begin following the steps provided in order to ensure a safe and successful pregnancy!

Finally, if you enjoyed this book, please take the time to share your thoughts and post a review on Amazon. It'd be greatly appreciated!

Thank you and good luck!

www.ingramcontent.com/pod-product-compliance
Lightning Source LLC
LaVergne TN
LVHW021745060526
838200LV00052B/3488